CONTENTS

INTRODUCTION

Have you ever watched a fly bumping repeatedly against the glass of a window as it tries to escape? Maybe you have tried to help it towards the open part of the window, only for it to frustratingly keep returning to its futile efforts to pass through glass.

Sometimes we are like that fly, wanting things to be different, but sticking with our habitual ways of thinking and doing things and not noticing how close we are to a way forward.

My interest in how we learn to think, feel and interpret our experiences has been sustained and informed over four decades of working with offenders in the community and prisons, and more recently with secondary school students.

This short book has two aims. Firstly, to encourage the recognition that how we feel is not who we are. Secondly, to briefly summarise a selection of practical theories, which I have found helpful in achieving freedom from some learned beliefs that can hold us back.

******

Until I mentored Joe (not his real name), I'd always assumed that everyone wanted to be happy. Joe is a teenager who prefers to be sad. He told me that he could remember occasions when he had felt happy, but the experiences associated with the loss of that fleeting feeling had been very painful, so now he settled for sad.
He felt out of his depth with life, had considered suicide, and was wary about relinquishing the security of sadness.

As he described recent experiences, and what they had led him to believe about himself, his preference for sadness made sense. Sadness was his safe place. He could be bullied, ignored or criticised, and it wouldn't affect his mood because it merely confirmed his low self-esteem. Praise or encouragement was a problem though, obliging him to respond in ways that demonstrated his unwillingness to believe anything positive about himself.

Joe's situation is not unusual. We all interpret our experiences in ways that defend our sense of who we are and the value we place upon ourselves.

Sadness is a natural response to experiences of emotional and/or physical pain. Generally, sad feelings fade when we resolve or come to terms with upsetting experiences. But, if we're unable to resolve what upsets us, there's a risk that sadness may deepen into depression *.

The distinction between sadness and depression is that those who feel sad are generally able to identify the cause of their sadness, whilst those experiencing depression report difficulty pinpointing an external reason or issue.
While a sad person remains aware of positive aspects of their life temporarily beyond reach, a person experiencing depression may have lost sight of anything positive in a fog of futility.

Unlike depression, feelings of sadness may be fleeting, and seldom interfere with social functioning.

For Joe, sadness had begun with feelings of alienation within his family, of being harshly judged, and fearful of where his increasingly frequent experiences of anger might take him. He described an occasion when he had attacked another boy, and had become alarmed at how repeatedly and mercilessly he had continued to punch him. Whilst he preferred the safety of sadness, anger still broke through and he would punch walls until his fist bled. The comforts of sadness could only be temporary. Joe needed to find a way out of the emotional prison in which he had sought refuge.

If Joe were to read this book, I hope that he would be able to begin considering some ways of becoming more aware, reflective, and skilful in managing the thoughts, emotions and feelings that give shape to his life.

I hope that you will too.

****

*Depression affects approximately 350 million people worldwide-with women twice as likely to develop the condition as men.

SECTION ONE: Reflections and Suggestions

Chapter 1 Worry

When we worry, it is usually because we want things to be different from the way they are. Whilst some practical worries, such as seemingly unmanageable debts, usually need expert guidance to resolve, most anxieties arise from learned ways of thinking and interpreting the things that happen.

If we get lost whilst walking in the countryside, we need to see more of our surroundings in order to find our way home. To do this, we climb a hill in order to get a better view.

Similarly, if we are feeling lost in some aspect of our life, we are more likely to find our way towards a skilful resolution if we raise our awareness, and look beyond our assumptions about who and what we are. This task is arguably urgent if we are settling for unhappiness as our "normal".

Personalities are formed by the ways in which our responses to events become habitual. We, and those with whom we interact, unthinkingly reinforce patterns of thinking, feeling and behaving. An obvious benefit of this is that we know what and who we like and dislike, and can relate to other people without too many surprises. It provides the comforts of the familiar and predictable. For those who are genuinely happy with how this has worked out for them, there is probably no need to continue reading unless it is to enable help to be offered to someone less fortunate.

If we are interested in making some changes to our habit based thoughts, feelings and assumptions, we can begin by examining how we make decisions, and how those decisions affect what happens next. For example:

- Worries arise because of how we think.

- Our ways of thinking are formed by our experiences **and the meaning we give to them.**

- The meaning we give to our experiences stems from our accumulated expectations and beliefs about ourselves (which we reinforce for fear of deviating from the consistency of what we believe to be our identity).

- Our opportunities are shaped by what we make things mean.

Worry arises via thoughts and feelings created by our experiences and what we believe they mean and say about us. These worries in turn feed back into our beliefs and expectations thereby ensuring the continuance of a vicious circle.

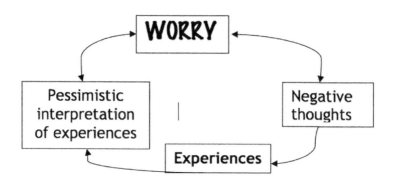

This vicious circle can be broken by understanding, and withdrawing the energy that powers it.

Worry is not an event that requires a response, but it may be possible to better understand it. In the same way that adverse weather conditions are the natural consequence of environmental causes, worry also has causes that can be understood.

By understanding how our minds work, and what influences our thoughts and moods, we can become more skilful in recognising worry as a natural (if undesirable) experience of the mind.

This is not to belittle worry or those who worry. Worry is a powerful mental experience that requires careful handling if we are to avoid being drawn into a debilitating vicious circle.

Experiences common to us all include:

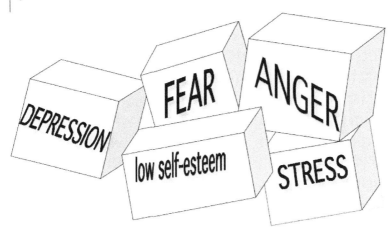

They can leave us feeling powerless and anxious, and we may settle for the "comforts" of sadness

we begin to deal with them differently.

We can start by thinking about this:
>   We are NOT **defined** by our feelings and emotions.
>   Who we are, is **having** the experience, but isn't the experience itself.

Because experiences are NOT who and what we are, we can CHOOSE whether they control our behaviour.

For Joe, worry was a pretty constant companion as it helped to maintain his sadness. He'd become stuck with a view of himself formed out of a need for consistency in his life. It had begun with clumsy, critical parenting that he'd wrongly believed meant there was something wrong with him. I remember another teenager, Dave, telling me that his father had thrown him downstairs when he was eight years old. Dave believed then, and when he was telling me nine years later, that it had somehow been his fault (it was more painful to find fault with his father). We had met because he had begun committing offences and was on a court order. His offending was, to him, inevitable as he'd come to believe he was a bad person, and offending is what bad people do. The "comfort" of consistency based on a seriously distorted interpretation of experience.

****

Suggested Exercise: Allow yourself two minutes to sit quietly alone each day. Observe the thoughts and feelings that arise without judging or attaching significance to them. After two minutes, quietly

say to yourself "despite these thoughts and feelings, I am okay".
How comfortable do you feel telling yourself that you are okay?
If you feel comfortable with it, that's fine.
If you feel uncomfortable with it, that's fine too, because it will change as you progress.   For now, it's a natural product of uncertainty.   Allow it, and let it go.

****

Q: Is everything we think and believe TRUE because we think it?
A: No

Chapter 2 MENTAL WEATHER

Feelings are like the
weather.

We experience the
weather and, although it
may affect our mood,
we don't take it
personally.

So, we might think of
feelings and emotions as a sort of weather passing
through our minds.
We experience them, but it's not who we are.

Who we are is having the experience just as we
experience getting wet in the rain without believing
that we are in some way defined by the rain.

The elements that contribute to our mental weather
include:
- The present situation.
- Past experiences.
- What our understanding of those experiences
  led us to believe about ourselves.
- The opinions and interpretations of others
  (actual or imagined).

In the same way that we can work with actual weather (umbrellas, sun screen etc.), there are strategies for coping with turbulent mental weather.

Although we can't control our emotions, we can learn to develop our awareness of them, how they arise and pass away, and recognize that we, the experiencer, remain Okay.

Recognising that we are Okay is important because when we feel Not Okay, we're more likely to do Not Okay things that will cause problems for ourselves and others.

Sometimes our negative thinking will insist that we're NOT Okay. When this happens we can avoid creating problems by considering how we would handle the situation if we did believe our self to be okay.
This will help us to access a more objective focus and increase the likelihood that we will act skillfully, and thereby minimize any negative consequences.

For more detail on developing positive thinking, see the chapter on Transactional Analysis.

Joe's mental weather was mostly grey and drizzly, but in some lessons at school he'd experience a sudden and violent storm that caused further erosion of his fragile self-esteem and good intentions.   He was relieved to return to the "comforts" of grey and drizzly.

****

Suggested Exercise: Take a few minutes to sit quietly and alone.   What sort of mental weather do you most commonly experience?
Are you able to see a connection between some mental weather and the meaning that you give to events at the time?

Q: How can we know that what we think and feel is not who we are?

A: Because who we are is able to observe and reflect upon the experiences (which are experienced by, but separate from the observer).

Chapter 3 BEING OKAY

When we feel down, memories of difficult or painful experiences from the past are likely to arise.
This is normal because our minds often seek out memories that confirm or reinforce the mood we are in. In this way we achieve a comforting consistency of mood and thought, but at the cost of prolonging negative feelings.

When you feel swamped by painful feelings, or are in the middle of a difficult experience, remind yourself ...

Despite this, I am OKAY

It's not that the experience is okay, it may be horrible, but YOU who are having the experience are okay.

If you find yourself thinking or saying "I am angry, unhappy", or whatever, making a conscious effort to change how you describe it can begin to lift the mood.

- Avoid "I am" because the feeling is NOT who you are. We are NOT defined by our feelings.
- Instead, create a little distance by thinking "this is anger, unhappiness, etc."
- Recognize the feeling for what it is, accept that it is an experience, but not **who** you are.
- Who you are is having the experience, but you are not the experience itself.

In this way you are less likely to do something you'll regret, and the feeling is likely to pass more quickly.

If the feeling persists, and you have a few minutes quiet time, you could try this:

Focus on the abdomen, and quietly say to yourself:
Breathing in, I accept my feeling.
Breathing out, I calm my feeling
Breathing in, I calm myself
Breathing out I smile.

Do it several times. You may need to remind yourself that you are doing it because you care about yourself, and are determined to manage old difficulties with new skills.

Take your time.
This is a new, mood lightening habit being developed.   There may be some resistance along

the lines of "I can't do this" ... "I don't deserve to feel better about myself" etc. ...
You **CAN** do this because you are basically OKAY.

Our basic okayness is like the sun behind clouds. It's always there, even on
gloomy days when all we
notice are the heavy
clouds of doubt, anxiety,
etc.

What we call our personality begins to take shape in childhood through interactions with parents, teachers, and others who care for us and have power over us.

By the time we become adults we have acquired a matrix of thinking and feeling patterns that operate as default programmes more complex than any found on a computer.
Sometimes, staying with the computer comparison, we pick up the equivalent of viruses that undermine our ability to function effectively.

Frequent feelings of anxiety, unless about a specific issue such as debt, illness, etc. is such a virus, and is mostly learned behaviour. Other people may have "learned" to behave in clumsy, selfish and even cruel ways.   It doesn't make it acceptable, but if we can see how it might have come about, we're more likely to respond in ways that avoid reinforcing negative thoughts, actions, and consequences.

The most helpful first step is to recognise that worry or anxiety is an experience, and not who we are. We can begin to deal with it by recognising the experience as something that comes and goes. It is impermanent so can't be our actual self.

Because anxiety (or anger, depression, etc.) is something that we experience only some of the time (even if it's a lot of the time) we know it isn't who we are because if it was, we wouldn't exist when it wasn't present.

This is Fred on Saturday and this is Fred on Monday

Fred's experience of contentment on Saturday is so different to his experience of anxiety on Monday that he feels like a different person.   But contented Fred and anxious Fred are of course the same Fred who is capable of *witnessing* each experience from his basic "Fredness".   When he recognises that he is witnessing changes in his **mental weather**, his ability to function improves, because the anxiety no longer controls him.

It's worth remembering that mental weather is mostly created by our experiences and what we make them mean.
The more we are able to recognise that some mental experiences are habits that can hold us back, the more we are able to experiment with new ideas and new directions in our lives.

When the actress Kate Blanchett told Michael Parkinson that "our lives are the result of our decisions" she neatly described the key to how we might help ourselves.

Joe rarely felt Okay.   Although he could recall the feeling (a little wistfully, I thought) it seemed like the memory of a holiday to an exotic place he knew he could never afford to visit again.

He had come to believe that he was fixedly defined by his feelings.   And this belief led him to behave in ways that caused the sort of things to happen that confirmed the "rightness" of those feelings.   A vicious circle.

Suggested Exercise: Tell yourself that you're Okay. How does it feel?
Do you believe you're Okay?

If you doubt that you're Okay, you might try the following exercise:

- Write a list of positive personal qualities (maybe ask friends for contributions if it seems a bit short)
- Read it to yourself several times each day for 21 days (the time it generally takes to create a new habit).
- If you find yourself forgetting or avoiding doing this, note that this is an effect of the old negative habit that *part of you* now wants to end.

If you find yourself resisting a positive view of yourself, relax; maybe return to it later. But, most importantly, recognize that your resistance is probably something that you have learned to do, a habit you've become accustomed to.   But it's not actually true, and holds you back.

Q: How can I achieve more control over my moods?

A: By reminding yourself that the mood is an experience, separate from whom you really are. Describe it to yourself using objective language ... "this is ..." rather than "I am ..." and the power of the (probably learned) mood will weaken.

Chapter 4 OPINIONS, DECISIONS AND CONSEQUENCES

What we believe about ourselves tells us what our experiences mean.   If we have a poor opinion of our self, we're more likely to expect little from life, and be unsurprised when things go wrong.   We may even blame ourselves for things that aren't our fault.

Our opinions arise from established beliefs and, if we have little belief in our own worth or that of others, our opinions will be shaped by those beliefs.

Our beliefs and opinions will inevitably contribute to the decisions we make, and the things we do or avoid doing.

And of course whatever we do or avoid doing will produce consequences.   And we will give meaning to these consequences according to our beliefs, and the merry-go-round continues (except of course, it isn't always merry).

Most of us want to attain or hold onto that feeling of security based on being able to correctly anticipate how things will turn out.

Generally we prefer the security of the familiar (sometimes settling for the "comforts" of sadness) because it is less threatening than the unknown, and provides a continuous sense of identity.

For some of us a belief in who and what we are is of such fundamental importance that we are prepared to put up with unhappiness for fear of losing that sense of a personal identity.
Our "comfort zone" might not be very comfortable!

And so we may travel through life clinging to a poorly constructed raft of second hand ideas and beliefs that
we
accumulated
in childhood.

Our raft takes us close to attractive places where people seem more content and capable, but when we consider leaving our raft and swimming to those places we become fearful that, without our raft of habitual beliefs, we will be swept away and drown (lose our sense of who we are).

Attachment to the "raft" of our identity, the mental constructs that contribute to a sense of self, can become an end in itself.

When the idea of detaching from some self-limiting "certainties" attracts us, it's time to examine how our thoughts, feelings and emotions are shaped.

Joe's "raft" was in pretty poor shape. He had lashed together a combination of his parent's critical comments, his perception of "unfair" school punishments, and a suspicion of once close friends whom he believed had abused his trust. Alone on his "raft" he experienced surges of impotent anger that sometimes frightened him. When I met him he was seeking refuge in the comfort of sadness as a rather desperate (and not entirely successful) way of keeping other emotions in check.

Suggested Exercise: Recall a story that you especially liked in childhood. Choose the character you liked the most, and maybe identified with. Take some time to write your version of the story solely from that character's experience.
When you've finished look to see if you are able to detect traces of beliefs and assumptions that you may have developed in childhood. Are they still present today?

Q: How might low self-esteem be improved?

A: By reflecting on how beliefs about self have been shaped by the behaviour of others, what we have decided that behaviour says about us, and challenging some of the negative stuff.

Chapter 5 THINKING

"If you think you can do a thing, or think you can't do a thing; you're right" Henry Ford.

Many of the world's great thinkers have concluded that **thoughts are often actions in rehearsal.** So, in order to change experiences that repeat with wearisome regularity, we begin by investigating the ways we think because our thoughts create and justify our actions.

If we do what we always do, we'll get what we've always got. If we want things to be different, we do things differently, beginning with how we understand and use our minds.

The psychologist William James rather caustically commented, *"Many people think they are thinking when they are merely rearranging their prejudices."*
Prejudices are generally learned behaviour. For example, research into racism found that young children learn this from their family and environment before, as adults, selecting anything that will serve as "evidence" to support the learned prejudice, and rejecting any facts that disprove it. If, as often happens, the racist becomes identity dependant on their prejudice, it's unlikely to be

shifted by rational argument as alternative views would feel threatening.

We start thinking long before we become interested in how it works. In childhood we begin to channel our experiences into a mental system that helps us to understand and interact with our environment. By the time we take a step back and consider how and why our minds work as they do, our thinking habits have developed, and with them, our personality. Because our personality relies upon those habits for a sense of continuity, we may be reluctant to let them go for fear of losing our identity; what we think of as "me".

This living, evolving combination of thought, emotion, and memory becomes, as Eckhart Tolle describes it in A New Earth, "me and my story", otherwise known as the ego.

If we come to believe that this ego is all there is to our identity, we are likely to get into difficulties, or create difficulties for others, or both. We can avoid this, and develop more skilful means of responding to events by continuing to investigate our mental processes.

Only rarely do we stop thinking, and even when we sleep our dreams suggest that a shadowy form of thinking is continuing to shape our beliefs about what and who we are, *and what we might expect from our lives.* Our expectations will influence our thoughts and actions, and will prove a significant factor in determining how our lives develop.

As we understand more of what thinking is, and why it works differently for different people, we see more clearly how opportunities are created or missed according to what we believe.

The meaning we give to an event or experience determines what we do next. Different people will respond differently to similar events according to what they have decided the event means to them.

Sometimes the reason we assume that an event means this or that is because we want to protect our beliefs from being challenged.

Those who are "comfortable" with sad and self-deprecating thoughts are likely to interpret experiences in ways that confirm their learned (and incorrect) belief that they are not okay.

Such interpretations will determine their decisions and actions.   These decisions and actions will, in turn contribute to new experiences and more clouds will obscure their basic, and for now lost, Okayness.

Those who generally feel okay about themselves and others will mostly do things differently.   Neither is more okay than the other, but different learned beliefs will always lead to different outcomes.
As Shakespeare had Hamlet say: "There is nothing either good or bad, but thinking makes it so"

Although the things we believe and do don't always make any *obvious* sense to others, there is usually an underlying purpose; some need that is being met. People who behave in ways that are repeatedly self-limiting are often unaware that, far from being accidental, their behaviour is satisfying an unconscious need.
By discovering what that need is, informed choices that can lead to a happier life become possible.

As Oscar Wilde wrote, in *The Ballad of Reading Gaol* "Nothing in the whole world is meaningless, suffering least of all".   By finding the meanings behind our suffering, we create the opportunity to make beneficial changes to how we respond to events as they arise in our lives.

Our behaviour, and the beliefs that create and justify it, is explained by George Kelly's Personal Construct Theory (see PCT chapter) as a continuous series of "experiments" designed to confirm our expectations, and thereby minimise any anxiety. But if anxiety or sadness IS what we expect, this theory suggests that we will seek, through our thoughts and actions, to ensure that's what we'll get.

Because our thoughts are frequently formed by what we believe and expect, it will be useful to examine those beliefs and expectations.   In order to do this effectively we keep in mind that, whilst our beliefs and expectations have a comforting familiarity, **they do not define us.**

Joe did a lot of thinking, in fact he recognised that the difficulty he had in sleeping was due to "overthinking".   Joe's thinking had become a form of self-torture as he kept revisiting his painful and self-deprecating interpretations of events at home and at school.   Without intending to, he had constructed a sort of mental prison from which he peered out at how other people were living their lives, and leaving him behind.   Happily, this would change as he applied new insights into his mental processes.

****

Suggested Exercise: Sit comfortably in a place and time when you won't be disturbed.
Float the question: "what's happening for me now?"
Thoughts or emotions will probably arise in your mind. Decide on a single word that sums up the thoughts/emotions (e.g. busy, eager, worried, etc.)
Watch for any judgements that may arise, and avoid (the habit maybe, of) attaching to them.

This simple task begins the process of watching the mind, and seeing what's happening for you from outside of the experience. i.e. objectively.

It may take a little practise, but by avoiding any urge to judge or react to whatever arises, you are likely to feel calmer and less resistant to the idea that you (the experiencer of thoughts) are basically okay.

****

Q: Why is the meaning we give to an experience so important?

A: The *meaning* we give to an event or experience is critical because it determines what we do next.
Different meanings lead to different responses.
These responses in turn shape new events, which we decide means .... and so it continues.

Chapter 6 FEELINGS AND EMOTIONS

Although feelings and emotions may be experienced as similar, their differences can briefly be summarised as:

Feelings are a state of mind sustained over time. From childhood, they develop from our experiences. The meanings that we give to those experiences arouse emotions, which consolidate into what we come to think of as our unique self.   When we seek to defend our feelings, we are defending what we believe to be our identity.

Simply put: feeling + meaning = emotion. **Emotions** are comparatively fleeting, and change as naturally as the weather.   In the same way that changes in the weather are driven by changes in air pressure and temperature, our emotions or moods are driven by events and what we decide they mean.

We begin to make sense of our environment and experiences from a very early age. As we attribute meaning to our experiences, we develop a network of feelings that form a template for interpreting future experiences. This (unique to the individual) network of feelings is like a country's topography. The mountains and valleys of feelings (shaped by experiences and what we think they mean) create the "weather" of our emotions.

The meaning we give to our emotions may deepen the "certainties" of our feelings and reinforce the meanings we give to our experiences.
This then confirms and maintains our mental "weather" system.

Although feelings and emotions are often considered different to thoughts, neuroscience (see reading list: Destructive Emotions) has demonstrated that the brain makes no clear distinction between them. Opinions and decisions arise from a combination of all three, with thoughts providing the words that we use to explain ourselves.

So, our feelings and emotions become a means of comforting ourselves with the creation of an identity.   Unfortunately, the emerging belief system is likely to be self-limiting because it will increasingly exclude alternatives that seem to challenge who we believe ourselves to be.

When people say things like "I'm the sort of person who always ..." or "I always think that ..." the underlying meaning is usually that they have chosen to imprison themselves in a speciously comforting certainty in order to maintain the reassuring "certainty" of a personal identity.

You are now sufficiently familiar with how Joe's mind works to guess that his feelings and emotions are seldom positive.

He had created an identity out of negative perceptions of himself and others.   The "comfort" of this was wearing thin though, and he told me that he had begun experimenting with self-harm and had considered ending his life.

****

Suggested Exercise: Connect & Strengthen is a continuation of Pause & Ask in the previous chapter. If we develop mindfulness by raising awareness of our body, mental turbulence is calmed and our basic Okayness resurfaces in consciousness.

Stand, with feet slightly apart and arms not touching your sides.

Beginning with your head, look for any tension, and move your attention slowly towards your feet, consciously relaxing any tense areas as you go.

Take your time, relaxing any tensions in jaw, shoulders (especially shoulders!), arms, buttocks and knees.

Widen your awareness to encompass your whole body.   Acknowledge any sensations along the way, but don't focus on anything specific.

Notice your breathing and, if you experience any area tensing up, focus on that, and let your awareness of breathing flow through the tense place.

Stay with this for 3 to 5 minutes at a time before gently coming out of the position, and noticing the change in body and mind.

Q: are feelings and emotions a problem?

A: No, they are natural experiences, but can be turned into problems if we mistakenly hold onto them and believe they tell us who we are.   We might treat them as a tree responds to wind.   It allows it to pass through.

Chapter 7 ANGER

Anger is a very powerful emotion that erupts into actions that lead to regret and can become habitual. It's often a vicious circle that looks like this:

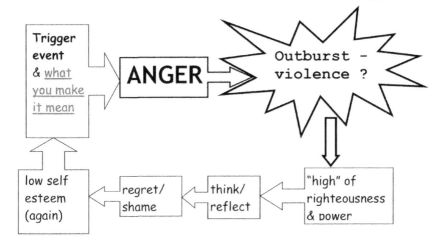

There's nothing wrong with *feeling* angry. Feelings aren't wrong, they just are. Feelings of anger and depression are clouds in our mental weather system. They arise and they cease, and we can CHOOSE whether to let them define us or not.
So, we'll experience feelings of anger, but we don't have to allow such feelings to control our behaviour.

Much of what we do is an attempt to manage our mood.

Anger may be triggered by a perceived threat to our self-esteem or being frustrated in pursuing some goal that is important to us. It's the most seductive of emotions and can be energising and exhilarating.

Escalating anger, unhampered by reason can erupt into violence. If we want to manage anger, we can begin by understanding how it arises.

Anger is a natural defensive response to threats, hurt and frustration. It can seem thrillingly empowering to someone more used to experiences of fragile self-esteem. Unfortunately, as indicated in the first diagram, the "high" of anger often results in a further erosion of confidence. This, via raised levels of stress, guarantees further angry outbursts and escalating feelings of pain, fear and shame.

STRESS can create adrenocortical arousal, lowering our anger threshold so that we experience events as a series of provocations, each triggering an excitable reaction that is slow to dissipate.

When we're STRESSED we're more likely to experience anger. When stressed, we're more likely to interpret events as threatening. Mostly they aren't, but when we believe they are, we'll do things that will cause us problems and make us even MORE STRESSED!

So ... when we realise that the volcano of anger might erupt, we need to quickly do some things that will help us to stay calm, and in control.

ANGER MANAGEMENT STRATEGIES

1. STOP METHOD

- When you feel yourself getting angry, say sharply to yourself 'STOP' (either loudly or under your breath) which means stop getting so worked up.

- Breathe deeply in through the nose and gently out through the mouth and develop a comfortable breathing pattern.

- Stay quiet for a while until you feel ready to continue with what you were doing.

2. DISTRACTION
- When you feel yourself getting angry, distract yourself from these feelings by thinking about something not to do with being angry.

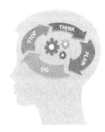

- Experiment with different ways, such as:

- Concentrate on what's happening around you. This could involve listening to other people's conversations, looking at what other people are wearing, what hairstyles they have. **Get your attention off yourself.**

3. SELF CALMING with the Tension Scale

Consider introducing the idea of a tension scale by drawing a ten point ladder or thermometer. Use the scale to calm angry feelings:

Picture the Tension Scale in your head. It may help to close your eyes.

Think about how angry you are. Is your anger a six or an eight, a five or a nine?

Now take a deep breath. Breathe out very slowly. As you breathe out, picture your anger coming down the Tension Scale.

when your anger is at a safe level, think about how you might resolve your problem.

Congratulate yourself for using good anger management.

OTHER THINGS YOU COULD DO

- Develop and practice assertiveness skills and social skills.
- Discuss your problems with someone you can trust. Work out a strategy to manage them in *ways that don't make them worse.*
- Take exercise when you feel yourself becoming angry.
- Walk away from situations you recognise as leading to trouble.
- Punch a pillow
- Check out just how bad it would be to be called names. Some people use names as a way of controlling others. It takes two (at least) to work, and it never makes anyone happy.

****

When you believe that other people's behaviour has caused you to feel anger, and you want to talk to them about it, use words with care. What we say can make things worse or better.

- Use "I" statements to say how you feel, and what you want.
- **Avoid "You" statements** because people will think you're blaming them.

It's a small change that achieves a big change in what happens next.

And finally, take care how you describe feelings of anger to yourself and others.

Avoid "I am angry" as this suggests that anger is a part of who you are.

Instead, think or say "I am experiencing anger".

Because anger is an experience, a form of mental weather as mentioned previously.

We get wet if we are out when it's raining, but experiencing wetness doesn't mean that we are wet as a person.

Anger is an experience that needs to be managed with care so that, like bad weather, it can pass without any lasting damage.

When things feel difficult, remind yourself again (say it to yourself under your breath) "Despite this, I am OKAY"

CALMING OTHERS with Cold Water Words

Other people's anger can be calmed by our response to them. Some examples of Cold Water Words are:
Uh-huh
Mmmm
You may be right
Does that bother you?
It sounds like you're feeling angry/hurt/sad
Tell me more
That must have made you feel awful!
You seem to be angry/disappointed/frustrated
Let's talk about it

And finally, it can help to consider the difference between assertive and aggressive use of language. Some people mistakenly interpret another person's assertiveness for aggression.   This mistake gives "permission" to respond aggressively thereby creating problems for themselves and others.

Examples of assertive:
"I feel"   "I don't like"   "I would like you to .."
"I'd like to talk about .." "I will not tolerate"

Examples of aggressive:
"If I were you .."   "forget it!" "you are .."

Joe generally seemed more depressed than angry on the occasions when we met.   But because depression is frequently the other side of the same "coin" as anger, I wasn't surprised when he described how his faux indifference to people and events could be swept aside by violent anger. Mostly this involved punching his bedroom walls, but he also described getting into a fight and being "unable" to stop beating an already defeated opponent.   That had frightened him.   He was becoming interested in considering new ways of approaching familiar problems.

Suggested Exercise: In addition to those described above, you could experiment with this, which further builds on the two previous chapter's exercises:

After becoming familiar and comfortable with the exercise in chapter six, experiment by adding this after you have focused your breathing.

- Bring to mind an event that recently aroused anger.
- Resist becoming submerged in the issues, and watch what is happening.
- What changes do you notice in your breathing, and your body?
- Are some areas becoming tense?
- Allow any physical changes, and focus upon the feeling of anger.   Just the feeling, the experience of it. Not the events that triggered the feeling.
- If you find yourself revisiting the events and what they meant for you, return to the feeling only.
- Allow the feeling of anger.   It's not wrong. It's a feeling; an experience that you are accommodating without doing anything.
- This is a very direct way of being with the emotions without blame or resistance.
- ... like holding a baby in your arms.   Attentive, careful, a little in awe.
- Allow yourself to feel what you feel. No judgment.
- Now, as you accept the feeling, expand your awareness to include your breathing again.

- As you become aware of your ability to accept the feeling without acting upon it, your emotional energy will become a source of warmth and goodwill to your self, your feelings, and to others who, like you, are mostly doing their best.

Q: If someone hits you with a stick, are you angry with the stick or the person wielding it?

A: Obviously not the stick, even though its impact on your body is what causes the pain.
But the hitter may, in a more complicated way, be like the stick.   He may be powered by mental illness, or misunderstandings that he believes to be true.   Of course, being hit, pain and anger arise immediately.   What we do next is vital if we are to avoid amplifying whatever is going on behind the scenes.

Chapter 8 HAPPINESS

Happiness, like worry, depression and love, is a feeling.   Because feelings develop out of the meaning we attribute to experiences, we have some responsibility for the feelings, but generally won't acknowledge this because what we make things mean becomes a reference point for interpreting events in our lives.

The meaning that we have given an experience arises by default from the meaning that we have given to previous, similar experiences.

By identifying and letting go of some of the self-limiting "certainties" that we have used to build the sense of "I'm this sort of a person", we free ourselves to experience more happiness.

It is of course easier to let go of something physically in our grasp than to abandon the comfort derived from the "certainties" that we have developed.   However, the process is similar. With both, we begin by considering the advantages and disadvantages of holding or letting go. If we are holding something that causes physical pain, the letting go is automatic.   We just let go. If however, it is a possession that requires time and money to maintain and we are beginning to doubt that it is worth the trouble, we consider the pros and cons of keeping or getting rid of it, make a decision and carry it out.

Although we may be aware that some of our acquired beliefs and feelings are causing us mental pain, there is no automatic letting go. Sometimes an underlying anxiety about our self-image and relationships with others can lead to the opposite. We may cling to the dysfunctional beliefs and feelings for fear  of losing our identity by letting them go. They may be painful, and we may feel unhappy, but at least they are familiar and reassuringly constant. Sometimes we pay for the "comfort" of the familiar in missed opportunities for greater happiness.

Any significant changes in our behaviour, requires courage because it involves stepping out of our comfort (or discomfort) zone into the unknown.

We make progress when we realize that clinging to the familiar can cause us to suffer. This is progress because it means that we have developed the courage and objectivity to begin investigating how our learned thinking and behaviour shapes our lives.

This is a powerful step forward because it is NOT learned behaviour. The decision to explore new ideas and ways of responding to the events that arise in our lives comes from that part of us that has always been okay.

It's like a cloudy day when the sun breaks through. Although we knew the sun was always there, the cloud affected our mood.

The part of us that is, and always was okay is like the sky, but sometimes the meaning we gave to our experiences has, like clouds, obscured the sky.

If we got too caught up in the drama of the clouds, and lost sight of our sky we may, like the fly unaware of the open window, have felt trapped.

Eckhart Tolle advises us to find that dimension within ourselves that is deeper than thought: "You are the sky; the clouds are what happens" They come and go, and we are freer and happier when we don't attach to them.

Joe recalled an experience of feeling happy, when playing with his cousins a year previously. Recalling that time he seemed to experience a sort of bereavement; the loss of someone he had once known and liked.

In the TV series "After Life", Ricky Gervais' occasionally suicidal character, Tony speaks of becoming "addicted" to negativity, and of feeling confused on the rare occasions when things go well. He says "When it all turns to shit, I go Oh, there it is" and feel back to "normal". Here we are shown the comforts of sadness as both bleak and potentially comedic.

****

Q: Who or what puts you under constraint/holds you back in life?

A: ??? ... your answer is likely to arise from a period of quiet reflection.

Chapter 9: CHILDREN: PARENTING & TEACHING

Whatever our age, there remains a part of us that is a Child (one of the three Transactional Analysis ego stated).
If we are a parent and/or a teacher, our interactions with children will be influenced by a combination of our ego states (Parent, Adult, Child) and our mood in the moment.

Our mood will often determine which of the ego states we operate from.   We will increase the skill and effectiveness of our interactions with children if we are alert to mood and the appropriateness of the ego state it has activated.
Children who can't read the emotions of others or express their own, constantly feel frustrated because they don't understand what is going on.   Making mistakes in the kind of emotional messages sent leads to unexpected reactions, and possibly getting rebuffed and wondering why.
A child who thinks he's acting happy, but is perceived as hyper or angry will be treated as he's perceived and won't know why.   Such children end up feeling that they've no control over how other people treat them.   They feel powerless, depressed and apathetic.

Emotionally malnourished children will often perceive neutral acts as threatening ones, and respond with the defensive habit of attack.

According to Dr. David Hamburg (psychiatrist and behavioural scientist) "From age 6 to 11 school is a crucible and a defining experience. A child who fails in school sets in motion the self-defeating attitudes that can dim prospects for an entire lifetime."

There is evidence that the emotions of prejudice are formed in childhood in sympathy to those of parents. The beliefs used to justify them come later as the developing adult selects only information that supports what has become a core construct (see Personal Construct Theory).

With IQ held constant, five year olds achieved better grades if their parents were good Emotional Intelligence (EQ) coaches.

Testing eight month old babies' outlook on life, paediatrician Dr. Brazelton offered two blocks to babies after showing them how he wanted them put together. The different actions and body language of these babies demonstrated that they had already learned a positive or negative self-view.

Parental behaviour likely to limit the child's development of Emotional Intelligence (EQ) includes:

1. ignoring child's feelings
2. inconsistent responses
3. contemptuous of child's feelings
Inconsistent responses to unwanted behaviour inevitably leads to the child escalating his/her behavioural "experiments" (see Personal Construct Theory) in an attempt to achieve a reassuring level of certainty.

The Austrian psychiatrist Rudolph Dreikurs (see suggested reading) developed Alfred Adler's work on the urge to power in working with children whose behaviour was challenging. He identified what he called four mistaken childhood goals

1. <u>Desire for undue attention</u>: a mistaken assumption that she only has significance when the centre of attention.
2. <u>Struggle for power</u>:   (to defeat the parent) punishment is a price worth paying for victory. Attempting to overpower a power drunk child is a grave and futile mistake as it will increase his belief that he is worthless unless he "wins" the battle.   In short, direct attempts to exert control is likely to cause the unwanted behaviour to escalate.

3. Retaliation and revenge: an escalation arising from discouragement and low self-worth. It becomes deeply self-fulfilling.
4. Complete inadequacy: a completely discouraged child gives up entirely.

In "Children: the Challenge", and "Happy Children", Dreikurs offers numerous examples and down-to-earth guidance on managing challenging behaviour in ways that help both child and parent.

Similarly, in a modern book aimed at helping teachers to avoid being drawn into an escalating war of attrition with challenging students, Paul Dix offers inspiring insights and guidance of use to teacher and parent alike.

Joe is a child, although as a teenager, he'd probably not choose that word to describe himself. He readily acknowledges that his behaviour is challenging, but mostly he focuses on what he perceives as the shortcomings of others. He frequently says that he avoids all but essential contact with his parents, and at school believes that he is unfairly singled out for punishment.
Despite this, he will say, from his cell of sadness, that he doesn't care. I avoid challenging this claim as his punctual attendance at our sessions suggests some motivation for change.

Suggested Exercise: (Maybe return to this after reading the chapter on Transactional Analysis)

If you are a parent or teacher, call to mind a difficulty with a child that seems to be stuck on repeat.   Think about which ego state (P,A or C) you are in when this happens, and where are you on the Okay Corral?   How might things change/improve if you worked at resolving the issue from a different ego state and/or from a different quadrant of the Okay Corral?

If you are a young person who regularly experiences the same sort of difficulty with a parent or teacher, consider some new responses that you could try out. As above, consider which ego state you're mostly in when the difficulty arises, and how things might be different if you made a conscious switch to a different one.

And a supplementary: Do you really want it to change, or is there some sort of comforting familiarity about the ritual?

****

Q: Generally, is there one ego state (P, A or C) that works better than the others?

A: No.   Each is appropriate to different situations. They can work well for us, ensuring empathetic and skillful relationships.   However, sometimes learned behaviour and/or fragile self-esteem can activate an inappropriate ego state (e.g. Critical Parent or Rebellious Child) and a difficult situation worsens.

WHEN YOU KEEP
CRITICIZING
YOUR KIDS, THEY DON'T STOP LOVING YOU.

THEY STOP LOVING THEMSELVES.

SECTION TWO: PRACTICAL THEORIES
Chapter 10 TRANSACTIONAL ANALYSIS (TA)

TA is a framework for understanding human behaviour, originally developed by Eric Berne. He had been through lengthy analysis and wanted to develop a faster more accessible method for people to get to grips with how attitudes and behaviours are formed.

TA explains how and why:
- our personalities develop as they do.
- we communicate with varying degrees of effectiveness.
- we behave in a variety of ways to get our needs met.
- we develop a unique belief system..

TA is broadly humanistic in its philosophical base, psychoanalytic in its concern with the way the past influences us in the present, and behaviourist in its emphasis on encouraging people to change as rapidly as possible.

This brief and simple introduction to TA will summarise some key words and concepts that can help to develop new ways of dealing with old difficulties. These concepts are interrelated; so it will probably be useful to read through, then read again so as to see the connections.
For more detail, please refer to the suggested reading list.

GAMES

Eric Berne's first, and best known book "Games People Play" described how much of our behaviour is unconsciously seeking "payoffs" from others that confirm what we already believe about ourselves. Usually these are beliefs about being NOT OKAY in some way (see "Okay Coral" below)
They can become compulsive and repetitive, and are "played" in order to get Strokes (see below) that keep us in our comfort zone, even if that comfort is a Racket feeling (see below) of quiet sadness.
"Games" are always played from the ADAPTED CHILD ego state (see below), and we can avoid initiating or colluding in Game playing by shifting to our ADULT ego state.

STROKES

In TA this word refers to the ways in which people actively recognize or acknowledge each other.
Strokes can be either positive or negative (we know which is which without having to think about it!)
They are sometimes (particularly when explaining them to children) called **WARM FUZZIES** and **COLD PRICKLIES** because of the feelings they arouse in us.

It is the type of **strokes** that we receive in childhood which begin to shape what we believe about ourselves, and expect from others. The origins of the comforts of sadness will sometimes be found here.

Our actions will often attract strokes that fit with the sort of person we have learned to believe ourselves to be.

Similarly, the sort of strokes that we give to others frequently reflects both how we see them, **and how we see ourselves in relation to them.** Which brings us to the ...

OKAY CORRAL

- + I am not OK You are OK Helpless/depressed	+ + **I am OK** **You are OK** **Happy/healthy**
- - I am not OK You are not OK Hopeless	+ - I am OK You are not OK Angry

Franklin Ernst developed this quadrant to demonstrate the different perceptions of self and others that we adopt according to circumstance and social interactions.   Our responses to situations will vary according to which segment our sense of self is occupying.

To reduce the risk of our responses in difficult situations adding to, rather than managing the difficulty, it's useful to regularly check out which segment we're in and (unless we're ++) proceed carefully.

EGO STATES & PERSONALITY DEVELOPMENT

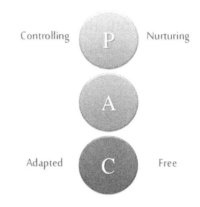

The Parent, Adult, Child (PAC) ego-state model in TA helps us to understand some basic underlying elements of our personalities.

An ego-state is a set of related thoughts, feelings, and behaviours at a given time.

• **Parent ego-state**: thinking and behaving like our parents or those who cared for us in childhood. It contributes to opinions, values, and setting limits on behaviour. Outwardly it may be expressed as controlling or nurturing behaviour.   Inwardly, old Parental messages and expectations continue to influence the inner CHILD.

- **Adult ego-state:** objective/rational thinking, using all available resources. It's not related to age. It functions by testing reality, considering probabilities, and deciding dispassionately.

- **Child ego-state:** thinking and emotions similar to our childhood. It contains recordings of our early experiences, how we reacted to them, and the "positions" that we took about ourselves and others

As the first ego state to develop, the **CHILD** is the more complex, containing a number of components.

*FREE CHILD: our spontaneous awareness of joy, feelings, sensations, and stimuli and our responses to them. Negative FC can be expressed as destructive, over-impulsive behaviour (e.g.violence and drug abuse).

*ADAPTED CHILD: includes the range of behaviours and responses that are shaped by the demands of parents when we were children. (please/thank you). Negative AC can be expressed as frequent feelings of anxiety, depression and guilt, or spending all the time pleasing others. OR frequent feelings of anger /frustration (may believe that the only way to get people to do what you want is to be angry).

*INTUITIVE CHILD (little professor): the unschooled wisdom of a child; responding to non-verbal messages and playing hunches. Highly creative. The emerging **ADULT** in the **CHILD**.

The **PARENT** begins as we take on the values, attitudes, and behaviours of parents or parent figures.

   *NURTURING PARENT: taking care of yourself and others.   Visiting a sick friend, having an early night when tired.   In excess you find your time getting swallowed up by the needs of others backed up by a sense of guilt if you don't respond.

   *CONTROLLING or CRITICAL PARENT: used well and properly we can be assertive (not aggressive) i.e. setting limits, giving instructions, chairing meetings etc.
Used badly we may find ourselves unable to delegate because we don't trust colleagues enough. We may be dominating in friendships and feel hard done by. We may become over-critical of ourselves, having internalised early critical messages full of **oughts, shoulds**, and backed up by guilty or anxious feelings.
   We need a good effective **PARENT** in order to make ethical and moral decisions, look after ourselves, and others.
   In conjunction with our **ADULT** we think about changing attitudes and values, and are able to adapt and respond appropriately.

The practical things that we learn as we grow contribute to the developing **ADULT**.   We learn to make decisions for ourselves based upon consideration of available information.

Over protective parenting can delay the development of a strong **ADULT**.   Children from over-protective or rejecting families can have difficulties in using their **ADULT**.   They may be indecisive, confuse feelings with thinking, and rely on **CHILD** emotions or **PARENT** opinions instead of **ADULT** thinking when making decisions or solving problems.

When our **CHILD & PARENT** get into an internal quarrel (do what you want V. do your duty) our **ADULT** can think things through, and sort out facts from feelings and opinions.

All the ego states are of equal value and, used mindfully, help build and develop fulfilling relationships and transactions with others.

Most people develop one ego state that is stronger or more pronounced in their personality than the others.   We tend to reinforce our own type of personality by choosing a lifestyle that fits in with it. e.g.

- caring professions or work involving authority: strong PARENT
- computing, accountancy, science, law: strong ADULT
- arts, media: strong CHILD

PAC PROBLEMS IN PERSONALITY DEVELOPMENT

Missing Adult: confusion between **wants** and **oughts**.

Missing Parent: little sense of right or wrong, unable to take care of self or others, or set boundaries around behaviour.
Missing Child: serious, thoughtful and dutiful, but no fun.

SCRIPTS
From an early age we develop ideas about who we are and what we want to be or do with our lives. Our experiences from birth to the age of seven or eight, and what we believe they mean, form our individual Script or life plan.

Sometimes the messages are positive, giving permissions :
> like yourself
> be happy
> develop your own personality fully

Sometimes the messages are restrictive or destructive, acting as prohibitions or injunctions that stunt emotional growth and development.
> don't have fun
> don't get angry
> don't expect much from life
> don't expect ever to be good enough

If you want to change your Script:
• 	Recognise that it probably arises from a decision based upon a childhood interpretation of events and Parental messages
• 	The decision of what to do with your life is yours alone.
• 	Recognise that you are free to make changes

according to what you want to achieve.

DRIVERS

Drivers are linked to Script beliefs, feelings and behaviours. Useful details can be found in TA Today (see recommended reading). Drivers are so called because they drive the beliefs that influence behaviour and shape the consequences that confirm the beliefs. They are deployed to keep us in our (sometimes uncomfortable) comfort zone of familiar experiences.

There are five Drivers, and most of us have a "favourite" that influences us more than the others.

Unconsciously (mostly) they are triggered by "I'll be okay if...."
1.   I'm Perfect
2.   I Please others
3.   I Try Hard
4.   I'm Strong
5.   I Hurry Up

There are particular words and gestures associated with each Driver (see TA Today). By discovering our "favourite" we can achieve release from unconscious Script based thinking and behaviour.

RACKETS

A Racket feeling is a "favourite" learned bad feeling.   It's familiar and we know the worst it can do.   Our Child ego state learns which of these feelings is the least uncomfortable to hold in a difficult situation.   Our Child learns what is permitted (e.g. if things are going badly at home, everyone gets short tempered, and it's okay to get angry) or what gets results in the form of wanted recognition Strokes.

Sometimes a Racket feeling is used to cover an authentic feeling.   For example, a little girl learns that in her family it's unacceptable to be angry, but okay to feel sad.   She received Strokes for managing her emotions in that way.   As an adult she may be in a situation where she is about to get angry with someone, perhaps being elbowed rudely on a crowded bus, but her Script triggers a conditioned reflex, and instead she bursts into tears.   This is the least uncomfortable feeling "allowed" by her Script.

Racket feelings include:
- embarrassed
- stupid
- bored
- guilty
- clumsy
- rejected
- anxious

There is much more of value in TA. If you find it interesting, I recommend dipping into the recommended reading.

I have found TA to be very useful when working with children as the concepts relevant to them are simple and easily understood. For example, they quickly understand how they mimic their parent's behaviour when encouraged to reflect on how they act with pets, younger siblings, etc.

Chapter 11 KELLY'S PERSONAL CONSTRUCT THEORY

George Kelly described how human behaviour can be seen as a series of experiments designed to test our beliefs in order to better anticipate the near future. Constructs provide a theoretical basis for anticipating future events based on the meanings we gave to earlier events.

A simple way of eliciting constructs is to think of three people you know, and consider a quality or characteristic shared by only two of them.   Then decide what the opposite is, and you have a construct.   A conceptual filter.

As an anticipated events happens, we continuously evaluate and modify our constructs in the light of outcomes.

Kelly referred to all of us as "scientists", developing expectations, testing them against outcomes, and modifying them accordingly.

These "experiments" may be distorted if the outcomes seem to contradict our core beliefs.

Example: If I believe that Arctic Airlines offers the best service in the world, and then have a dreadful trip where everything goes wrong, I do one of two things: either I adapt my construct system, altering my feelings about them in the light of our experience; or I immunise my construct system, with thoughts like They must have been having a really bad day, or Yes, but the airport was so overcrowded they didn't stand a chance.

Whether I adapt or immunise depends on a number of things: how open I am to new information, how much it matters to me to maintain my belief in the superiority of Arctic Airlines, how important it is to me to have a lot of information about airlines anyway.

Our construct systems influence our expectations and perceptions.   Also, if we're expecting Arctic Airlines to treat us well, we probably get on the plane in a better mood than we would on an airline which gave us poor treatment last time. If our experience is that Arctic's cabin staff always smile when they meet us, we probably board the plane with a smile ourselves. We might not notice when Arctic's service fails to live up to standard, but pay attention when it happens with the other airline. Because our construct system reflects our past experience, it also influences our expectations and behaviour.

Some constructs, and some aspects of our construct systems, are more important that others. The airline example repeats in every area of our experience. We feel, think, and behave according to our construct system; we adapt our constructs, immunise them, or have them confirmed.

Some of our constructs - those which represent our core values and concern our key relationships - are complex, quite firmly fixed, wide-ranging, and difficult to change; others, about things which don't matter so much, or about which we haven't much experience, are simpler, narrower, and carry less personal commitment.   Your construct system is your "truth" as you understand and experience it - nobody else's:

Construct systems are not objective truths.
When we meet someone whose construct system is different from our own - especially if we don't like it, or think it's wrong - we might try confronting them with opposing opinions or evidence.   Then we'll get frustrated if they immunise their constructs against our facts or opinions instead of adapting them.
More helpful is to begin by accepting that their system has worked, more or less, for them so far, and that if it is different from ours that's because they've had different experiences, and see different things as important.
If we reflect upon our own construct system, and how it's working out for us, we might gain new insights into what core beliefs (Scripts in TA language) it's serving.

We begin developing our constructs during childhood.

The constructs created by parents about their children will be perceived and used by the children as reference points in a confusing world.

Children initially "borrow" their parents constructs, and move on to develop their own systems. Loosely structured at first, then more tight and systematic during their teenage years.

A comparison of disturbed and ordinary boys found that the disturbed were less able to anticipate the subtleties of social situations. They had too few interpersonal constructs, resulting in social clumsiness.

Parental inconsistency will impair psychological growth as the child is confused and her/his ability to successfully anticipate/construe is limited.

Troubled teenagers use more constructs focussed on behaviour and less on the subtleties of personality.

- Their social behaviour is clumsy because of their underdeveloped construing skills, and this can reduce their ability to enjoy socially fulfilling experiences.
- Limited ability to interpret or empathise with the behaviour of others can lead to mutual rejection and hostility.
- He/she can only interact effectively with those whose behaviour is construed as meaningful.
- This can lead to isolated selfishness and heightened anxiety.
- There is often a tendency to increasingly invest in the fantasy of fictional heroes, which become a sort of ideal self.

- Challenging behaviour may be a clumsy attempt to discover where the boundaries are, if inconsistent parenting did nothing to help shape this important construct.

A settled, socially inclusive community may not be able to construe the constructs of young people whose behaviour is challenging or difficult. His/her behaviour won't make any sense, and is simply annoying.

The Manual for Repertory Grid Technique (suggested reading) outlines methods for eliciting constructs. Using a Repertory Grid can clarify the gaps between how someone sees themself compared to how they would like to be. They may then use these insights to experiment with new behaviours, which will result in new (and probably more rewarding) outcomes.

Such experiments are called Fixed Role Therapy. A conscious effort is made to try new ways of responding to familiar difficulties. This will create unfamiliar outcomes, which will create new constructs. If the outcomes are found to be positive, this will reinforce changes that began as an experiment.

Chapter 12 EMOTIONAL INTELLIGENCE (EQ)

In his book on the subject (see recommended reading), Daniel Goleman argues that the common view of intelligence is too narrow. Our emotions contribute significantly to our thinking and decision-making. Learning to manage our emotions begins in childhood, and is heavily reliant upon our parent's abilities to model skilful methods.

Our EQ begins to develop during childhood and continues throughout our lives. Depending on the things we learn to believe about ourselves and others, EQ can help or hinder our attempts to deal with life's difficulties*.

Emotional Intelligence helps us to:

1. Develop self-awareness, and understanding of our emotions
2. Manage our emotions

3. Motivate ourselves
4. Recognize and have empathy for other people's emotions
5. Handle relationships through skill in managing other people's emotions

Much of what we do, especially how we react to perceived threats, is an attempt to manage our moods.   By developing our Emotional Intelligence we are better able to respond to threats or difficulties without unintentionally making things worse.

Without sufficient EQ, worries can become self-fulfilling prophesies, propelling us towards the predicted disaster.   In such circumstances, no matter how intellectually intelligent we may be, anxiety can undermine our intellect and lead to clumsy decisions.

Feeling swamped by dreadful, out of control feelings is described in EQ as "flooding". Whatever is said to a "flooded" person is likely to be distorted so as to fit with the dominant, negative emotional mood.

Flooding begins at about ten beats per minute above the normal heart rate. At 100+ beats per minute the body is pumping adrenaline and other hormones, which keep the distress high for some time. With emotions so intense, perspective so narrow, and thinking so confused, there is no possibility of considering another persons viewpoint or settling things in a reasonable way. The more often we are in situations that trigger "flooding", the lower our "flooding" threshold becomes, and the less skilful our defensive avoidance tactics.

As we read about EQ we increase it because we are raising our awareness. We can:

1. Consider our performance against the five ways EQ can help (see above). We don't have to discuss what we are doing with anyone, but it's important to be honest with ourselves as we reflect upon our weaknesses and strengths.
2. Consider how we might increase our EQ. For example, by increasing self-awareness of emotions by thinking back over occasions when they have felt overwhelming. Give names to different emotions, remembering that they are an experience, but do not define us.
3. If we've previously made the common mistake of identifying with our emotional experiences, naming the emotions and thinking of them as passing experiences (mental weather) will help. E.g. this is anxiety, anger, etc. rather than "I am anxious". A subtle difference, but

one, which inserts a small gap between us and the experience. This strengthens the second of the five EQ skills.

4. Consider what motivates us, and what seems to persuade us not to bother. If that were a friend, what advice might we offer?

5. Watch how other people's emotions affect their behaviour. Give names to their apparent emotions, and consider the feelings that their emotions arouse in you, and how those feelings might affect how you would relate to them.

6. Having recognized and named some of your own and other people's emotions, take some time to think about how you might better manage an unavoidable relationship (e.g. student/teacher) with someone you find difficult.

CONCLUSION

When we look carefully at the lives of others, the decisions they make, and the way things are working out for them, we may see some of the how and why that they do not see.

Similarly, when others look at us they may also see what we have yet to recognize and understand.

By quietly raising our awareness to the meaning behind what we and others say and do, we can increasingly step outside of learned ways of thinking and being that have outlived any usefulness they might once have had.

Comforts come in many forms. If we default to criticism of the unusual or damaging refuges from which others draw a little comfort (sadness, alcohol, drugs, etc.) we may miss opportunities to share the basic Okayness at the heart of us all.

I hope that some of the observations and borrowed theories in this short book will encourage us to use the umbrella of mindfulness in order to cope with some of the mental weather that is an inescapable aspect of our lives.

Many paths lead from
the foot of the mountain.
But at the peak
we all gaze at the single
bright moon.

-Ikkyu-
1394-1481

John Harvey 2020

RECOMMENDED READING

General
- Destructive Emotions: Daniel Goleman & The Dalai Lama
- Happy Children; the Challenge for Parents: Rudolph Dreikurs
- Children; the Challenge: Rudolph Dreikurs
- Blame My Brain (the amazing teenage brain revealed):   Nicola Morgan
- When the Adults Change, Everything Changes: Paul Dix

Transactional Analysis
- Games People Play: Eric Berne
- TA Today: Ian Stewart & Vann Joines
- What Do You Say After You Say Hello?: Eric Berne
- Games Alcoholics Play: Eric Berne
- TA for Tots: Alvyn M Freed
- TA for Kids: Alvyn M Freed
- TA for Teens: Alvyn M Freed

Personal Construct Theory
- Inquiring Man: Bannister & Fransella
- A Manual for Repertory Grid Technique: Fransella & Bannister

Emotional Intelligence
- Emotional Intelligence: Daniel Goleman

Printed in Great Britain
by Amazon

24194019R00047